THE FBI STORY

HOW TO BECOME an FBI AGENT

By William David Thomas

MASON CREST PUBLISHERS

Produced in association with Water Buffalo Books.
Design by Westgraphix LLC.

MASON CREST PUBLISHERS INC.
370 Reed Road
Broomall, Pennsylvania 19008
(866) MCP-BOOK (toll free)
www.masoncrest.com

Printed in the United States of America

First Printing

9 8 7 6 5 4 3 2 1

Library of Congress Cataloging-in-Publication Data

Thomas, William David.
    How to become an FBI agent / William David Thomas.
        p. cm. — (The FBI story)
    Includes bibliographical references and index.
    ISBN 978-1-4222-0571-6 (hardcover : alk. paper) — ISBN 978-1-4222-1378-0 (pbk. : alk. paper)
    1. United States. Federal Bureau of Investigation—Juvenile literature. 2. United States. Federal
Bureau of Investigation—Vocational guidance. 3. Law enforcement—United States—Juvenile literature.
4. Criminal investigation—United States—Juvenile literature. I. Title.
    HV8144.F43T493 2009
    363.25023'73—dc22   2008048093

Publisher's note:
All quotations in this book come from original sources and contain the spelling and grammatical
inconsistencies of the original text.

CONTENTS

1 The FBI's Most Wanted

Melanie Wood is a college student in Virginia. She works part-time in a sandwich shop and lives in a run-down apartment above it. One Tuesday evening she is in the laundromat down the street, folding the clothes she has just taken out of the dryer.

A Dangerous Town

A tall, thin man with a wild look in his eyes bursts through the front door. He leaps over a table, scattering Melanie's laundry onto the floor, and throws one arm around her neck. Behind him, another man and

Hogan's Alley is a made-up town on the grounds of the FBI Academy. No training experience will ever match what agents encounter on the job. But everything about Hogan's Alley—including people playing criminals—is as lifelike as possible in order to create a realistic environment for new agents and veterans alike.

a woman run into the laundromat, pointing pistols at Melanie and her attacker.

"Freeze!" they shout. "FBI!"

The tall man presses a gun against the side of Melanie's head and screams, "Drop the guns or I'll kill the kid. I swear I'll kill her!" He starts walking slowly backwards, dragging Melanie with him.

It's another rough night in Hogan's Alley, the most crime-ridden town in America.

A Lot to Learn

The little town of Hogan's Alley is actually fake, but it's a very real part of the training academy for the Federal Bureau of Investigation—the FBI. Every day its streets are full of bank robbers, drug dealers, and terrorists. All of those "criminals" are instructors or actors. And while the action in Hogan's Alley is intense and varied, it's only a small part of the instruction that goes on at the Academy. Trainees have a lot to learn before they become members of the most famous law enforcement agency in the world.

First, a Little Bit of History

In 2008, the FBI marked its 100th anniversary. The organization's name, composition, and mission have all changed dramatically over those years. But how—and why—did the Bureau begin?

Today it seems obvious that laws made by the U.S. government are the most powerful in the land. One hundred years ago, however, that was not the case. State and local laws were much more important then. Law enforcement was often limited to a county or state. For example, if a man stole money in Ohio, the police could not chase him into Kentucky. They had no authority in another state. And Kentucky police might not be able to arrest the thief because he had not committed a crime there.

"The Special Agents"

President Theodore Roosevelt believed that the **federal** government needed to take a stronger role in law enforcement. He asked his **attorney general**, Charles Bonaparte, the man in charge of the U.S. Justice Department, to do something about it. In 1908, Bonaparte put together a group of 34 men to investigate crimes that crossed state lines. Many of these crimes involved banking and land **fraud**. The group had no name. They were simply referred to as "the special agents."

Spies and Bootleggers

In 1909, the group was officially named the Bureau of Investigation. Within a few years, the number of agents grew to more than 300. Field offices were set up in cities across the country.

During World War I (1914–1918), the Bureau's agents investigated foreign spies. The 1920s were the years of "**Prohibition**," when it was illegal to make, sell, or import alcoholic beverages in the United States. Criminals knew they could make money dealing in illegal liquor. The Bureau worked to stop those dealers, who were known as "bootleggers."

A New Name and a New Mission

In 1924, J. Edgar Hoover was named Director of the Bureau of Investigation, a post he held until his death in 1972. Under Hoover's leadership, the Bureau became much more professional. Formal training for new agents began. The Bureau became the central location for criminal fingerprint records in the United States. In 1932, the Bureau of Investigation was renamed the U.S. Bureau of Investigation, but only for about a year. Its name would change in 1933 to the Division of Investigation. In 1932, the Bureau also set up its first technical lab, known simply as its Crime Laboratory.

FAST FACTS

The first Justice Department investigators were just called "special agents." The name stuck with them. Today, these men and women may refer to each other as simply "agents," but officially they are FBI special agents.

J. Edgar Hoover is shown in the early and later years of his career as Director of the FBI. For decades, Hoover was, more than any single individual, the "face" of the FBI.

Crime became more violent in the 1930s. The era of prohibition spawned the era of gangsters, most of them involved in running illegal businesses and prostitution rings, as well as selling illegal alcohol and drugs. With increased competition for this kind of business, criminals became bolder in their efforts to eliminate that competition. Most of the gangsters shot and killed one another. Still, people were becoming increasingly fearful that growing mob violence—plus an increase in highly publicized kidnappings and crimes by bank robbers such as John Dillinger and Clyde Barrow and Bonnie Parker—would spread and threaten ordinary citizens. New federal laws gave the Bureau more authority, and in 1934

In the 1920s and 1930s, gangsters such as (top row) George "Machine Gun" Kelly and Charles "Pretty Boy" Floyd and (bottom row) Bonnie Parker and Clyde Barrow (known simply as Bonnie and Clyde) were given names and reputations that became part of the popular culture of their day. They were also ruthless killers—and the objects of manhunts by the Bureau and dozens of other law enforcement departments.

special agents were authorized to carry firearms for the first time. In 1935, the agency's name was officially changed to the Federal Bureau of Investigation—the FBI.

When the United States entered World War II (1941–1945), the FBI's main mission was protecting defense industries and catching spies and **saboteurs**. The Bureau also began stationing agents in U.S. embassies in foreign countries. These agents were called legal attachés, or "legats." Today they still work closely with foreign law enforcement agencies.

From Communists to Computers

After World War II, **communism** was seen as a major threat to the United States. Special agents searched for communists in the government and in technical and defense businesses.

During the 1960s, many new laws were passed to protect the **civil rights** of African Americans. The Bureau played an important role in protecting those rights and investigating crimes against African Americans and others who were targeted by hate groups.

In the 1970s, **undercover** FBI agents infiltrated organized crime families in the United States. They arrested many members of "La Cosa Nostra," often called the Mafia. When

One way that the FBI has helped control the spread of organized crime has been by infiltrating the mob. In this photo, agents transport an associate of a mob family from FBI headquarters.

illegal drugs became a serious problem in the 1980s, the FBI worked closely with the Drug Enforcement Agency (DEA) to stop drug smugglers and investigate their financial transactions.

As the use of computers grew in the 1990s, so did computer crime. Many of these **cyber crimes** involve **identity theft** and swindling people out of money. Others involve crimes against children through online child pornography and schemes to gain children's trust online for the purpose of meeting them and sexually abusing them. Bureau teams were organized to combat these new threats.

Terrorism

On September 11, 2001, the Bureau again took on an added mission. After the terrorist airline hijackings that led to the crash of a plane in Pennsylvania and attacks on the World Trade Center in New York City and the Pentagon near Washington, D.C., fighting terrorist attacks became one of

Most Wanted Terrorists

MURDER OF U.S. NATIONALS OUTSIDE THE UNITED STATES; CONSPIRACY TO MURDER U.S. NATIONALS OUTSIDE THE UNITED STATES; ATTACK ON A FEDERAL FACILITY RESULTING IN DEATH

USAMA BIN LADEN

Aliases: Usama Bin Muhammad Bin Ladin, Shaykh Usama Bin Ladin, The Prince, The Emir, Abu Abdallah, Mujahid Shaykh, Hajj, The Director

DESCRIPTION

Date of Birth Used:	1957	Hair:	Brown
Place of Birth:	Saudi Arabia	Eyes:	Brown
Height:	6'4" to 6'6"	Sex:	Male
Weight:	Approximately 160 pounds	Complexion:	Olive
Build:	Thin	Citizenship:	Saudi Arabian

Even before the attacks of September 11, 2001, al-Qaeda leader Osama bin Laden had been linked to other terrorist actions targeting U.S. citizens and officials. His name was placed on the FBI's Ten Most Wanted Fugitives list in 1999.

FAST FACTS

James E. Amos (shown at left) was the first African-American special agent. He started work in 1921. During World War II (1941–1945), he helped break up a ring of foreign spies.

the FBI's top priorities. Today, the Bureau has dramatically increased its **intelligence** and **counterterrorism** activities.

Today's Priorities

The Bureau's "What We Investigate" Web page (http://www.fbi.gov/hq.htm) lists the Bureau's current priorities. As of early 2009, the top three were all grouped under the heading of "National Security Priorities":

1. Counterterrorism: to protect the United States from terrorist attack.

2. **Counterintelligence**: to protect the United States against foreign intelligence operations and **espionage** (spying).

3. Cyber crime: to protect the United States against crimes ranging from identity theft and invasions of privacy to child pornography and other online crimes against children, intellectual theft (stealing and using other people's music,

Credit card fraud can start with an act as simple as providing your card number to someone who offers you nonexistent goods or services online. Other kinds of fraud begin with a victim providing a Social Security number or other identifying information. This can lead to identity theft and the illegal acquiring of credit cards in the victim's name. All of these crimes are targets of the FBI's Financial Crimes Section, which deals with white-collar crime.

books, photography, or movies for profit), and fraud (a way of profiting from deception or misrepresentation of oneself in financial dealings).

Other priorities were grouped under the heading of "Criminal Priorities," and they include the following: public corruption, civil rights, organized crime, white-collar crime, and major threats/violent crime.

The Most Wanted Skills

As the Bureau's priorities change, the skills needed by its agents change as well. The Bureau's Web site lists "critical skills" that it looks for in new agents. Some of them may surprise you.

Accounting. Nearly every crime involves money. It is stolen. It is counterfeited. It is used to buy drugs, weapons, and explosives. Tracing the flow of money between people, banks, states, and countries is one of the Bureau's biggest jobs. They want people who are experts at it. "We use financial investigative techniques to audit books and seize assets," says Jim Pledger, a long-time veteran of the FBI. "It's the best way to put the dopers behind bars."

Computer science and information technology. The FBI is probably the most technically sophisticated law enforcement agency in the world. The Bureau's extensive computer systems are one reason. These systems allow agents to track telephone records, match fingerprints, find and compare photographs of people, study financial records, and much, much more. The

Rapid advances in computer technology have opened up a whole field of employment for future agents that was not even imagined only a few decades ago.

FBI needs people who can use, maintain, update, and protect its computer systems. Criminals use computers, too. Cyber crime is on the rise. The Bureau needs agents who understand computer systems so they can find and arrest cyber criminals.

Foreign languages. The FBI needs people who can read, write, speak, and understand foreign languages. During World War II, the Bureau needed experts in German, Italian, and Japanese. During the **Cold War**, it needed people who could handle Russian, Korean, and Chinese. Now the Bureau needs people who are fluent in the languages of South Asia and the Middle East.

MEN IN THE BUREAU

ne time in the Bureau's history, only women were secretaries or sts. Things have changed. Today, FBI actively seeks women to me special agents. As the eau's Web site notes:

n many cases, women pos-
sess different analytical
skills, approach problems dif-
erently, and have different
alents and abilities than do
men. These different skills,
approaches, and talents often
spell the difference between
success and failure on a case
or investigation. We have
ound that investigative
eams composed of a blend of
emale and male special
agents are much more effec-
ive at bringing complex
nvestigations to a speedy
and successful resolution.
Female special agents have
proven to be a
remendous asset
o the FBI.

ners such as this, en from the FBI's b site, demon-
te the Bureau's
nmitment to
ruiting a diverse
ce of agents.

Law. Many special agents have law degrees. J. Edgar Hoover himself was a lawyer. The Bureau is, after all, charged with enforcing feder-al laws. Knowing those laws, and how they apply to many situations, is important. That knowledge helps agents investigate crimes, make arrests, and testify in court.

Police and Soldiers. Experienced police officers and detectives have already been trained in some of the skills that special agents need. Pilots, weapons experts, intelligence analysts, and other people from the military have skills that are important to the Bureau.

The Most Wanted People

Those are some of the critical skills the FBI wants. But what kind of people does the Bureau want most? It wants men and women of all races and religions. It wants people who are young, but mature, who are intelligent, educated, and physically fit. It wants people who are well-spoken, courageous, and unfailingly honest. And the FBI wants—in fact, demands—people who are loyal to each other, to the Bureau, and to the United States.

If you are one of those people, and if you have or can acquire any of the critical skills needed, you can apply to become an FBI special agent. And what will you get in return? A now-serving special agent (pictured below) said this:

> This is truly an opportunity of a lifetime, to be part of a greater cause. It's about challenging and being challenged. You are entrusted with the nation's security. This job isn't about money. No amount of money could buy you the kind of experience, access, or pride you will have as an agent.

CHAPTER 2

Paperwork, Polygraphs, and Push-ups

Criticized since the attacks of September 11, 2001, for not having enough employees who were fluent in foreign languages and for not quickly upgrading its computer systems, the FBI announced in January 2009 that it was launching one of the largest hiring campaigns in its 100-year history. The openings it publicized were for 850 special agents as well as 2,100 other professional staff. According to FBI

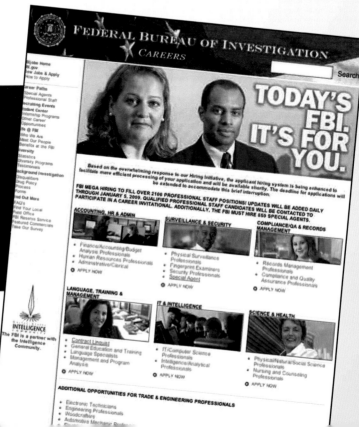

This is how the FBI's Web site on careers looked in January 2009, when the Bureau announced an ambitious campaign to hire nearly 3,000 new employees.

Assistant Director John Raucci of the Human Resources division, these openings were in such key areas as computer science, languages, finance and accounting, and physical **surveillance**. Reflecting the high priority that the Bureau now gives to national security, Raucci had this to say of the new openings:

> We're also looking for professionals in a wide variety of fields who have a deep desire to help protect our nation from terrorists, spies, and others who wish us harm.

If it sounds as if there might be a job for you among those that currently keep about 12,800 agents and 18,400 other FBI employees busy—or if you want to think about a career in the FBI someday—read on.

How Should You Begin?

Let's start with the easiest part. To even be considered as a potential FBI special agent, you must:

- be a citizen of the United States;

- be between the ages of 23 and 37; and

- have a four-year college degree, preferably in one of the Bureau's critical skills areas.

If you meet those basic qualifications, the process of becoming a special agent is still long and very competitive. The FBI is an elite agency. Its standards are extremely high, both mentally and physically. And if you want to try it, you have to start at a computer.

THE FBI SPECIAL AGENT HIRING PROCESS

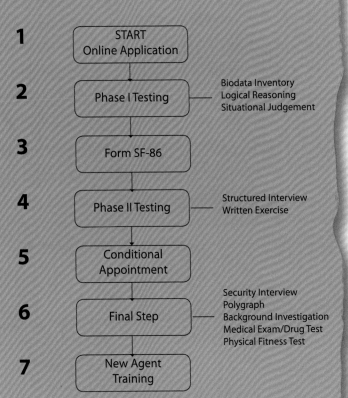

1 START / Online Application

2 Phase I Testing — Biodata Inventory / Logical Reasoning / Situational Judgement

3 Form SF-86

4 Phase II Testing — Structured Interview / Written Exercise

5 Conditional Appointment

6 Final Step — Security Interview / Polygraph / Background Investigation / Medical Exam/Drug Test / Physical Fitness Test

7 New Agent Training

The Online Application

The only way you can apply to the FBI is through the Internet. First go to www.fbijobs.gov and click on "Apply for a Job as an FBI Special Agent." At the top of the first page, you'll be told which skill areas the FBI wants most at the present time (remember, the Bureau's needs do change). Then you have to enter your ZIP code. That's because your application will be processed through the FBI field office closest to you.

The application form itself is long, with lots of questions about where you've lived, your education, military service, and work history. Part of the form reminds you that you'll have to move anywhere the Bureau wants you to go. You're asked about your willingness to carry and use firearms. There are questions about criminal convictions, past drug use, and membership in certain organizations. Finally, you must agree to a background investigation, a medical exam and drug-use test, and a polygraph (lie detector test).

Your application will be reviewed by a special agent in the nearest FBI field office. If you are qualified, you will be notified and scheduled for Phase I Testing.

Phase I Testing

These written tests take about four hours and are given only at FBI field offices. There are three different tests. One is called the Biodata Inventory. It asks questions about your behavior, your judgment, and how you relate to other people. The second test, the Logical Reasoning Test, checks your attention to detail and your ability to evaluate information and to make decisions based on that information. In the third test, the Situational Judgment Test, you are given a set of circumstances and choice of things you might do. You are asked to judge the effectiveness of each of the courses of action.

FBI field offices, such as these in Chicago, Pittsburgh, and San Juan, Puerto Rico, are where most candidates undergo testing.

PHASE I TEST QUESTIONS

These sample questions were taken from the FBI Web site. If they seem diffi-cult, remember that you need a four-year college degree before you can even take these tests.

From the Biodata Inventory:

How often are your library books overdue?
To what extent have you enjoyed being given a surprise party?
In the past year, how many times have you thrown something when you were angry?

From the Logical Reasoning Test:

Whenever an investigator is involved in an intelligence operation, he or she is required to examine multiple hypotheses, thus avoiding the quick pursuit of only one path, which could turn out to be incorrect. In a recent terrorism case, which thus far has proved to be exceptionally complex and remains unresolved, several hypotheses were initially generated about the suspects, conspirators, motives, and implementation of the terrorist act. Most of these hypotheses have been disproved.

From the information given above, it can be validly concluded that

A) in any intelligence operation, an investigator who generates more than one hypothesis is more likely than not to succeed

B) at least one of the hypotheses generated for the terrorism case mentioned above is not likely to be disproved

C) if an investigator is not required to examine multiple hypotheses about a case, then he or she is not involved in an intelligence operation

D) whenever an investigator fails to solve a case, it can be assumed that, most probably, he/she failed to generate more than one hypothesis about the case

E) there are at least some investigative operations, other than those concerned with intelligence, that do not require the investigator to form more than one hypothesis

[The correct answer must be chosen from one of the options given above. According to the text following these sample responses, the correct answer is C.]

From the Situational Judgment Test:

Your direct subordinate, who is returning to school full-time in three weeks, has a very negative attitude toward the company. She was counseled about it before, but her negative attitude continues. She is now beginning to be late for work and is showing disrespect to you and other staff. How effective is each of the following actions you could take?

A) Tell her that she is still an employee for three more weeks and can still be fired.

B) Dock some of her pay.

C) Try to get to the bottom of her bad attitude; find out if there are any problems that can be dealt with.

D) Counsel her one last time but ensure her that next time serious actions will be taken.

[The applicant is instructed to indicate the level of effectiveness of each of the above actions according to a scale of 1-2 (low), 3-5 (moderate), or 5-6 (high).]

There are no number or letter grades given on the Phase I tests. You either pass or fail. If you pass, you'll be invited to continue in the application process.

Form SF-86

If you pass Phase I testing, you'll have to fill out SF-86, the Questionnaire for National Security Positions. The form is 10 pages long. It has questions about your past work, foreign travel, your money, your relatives, friends, and drug and alcohol use. It also gives the Bureau permission to check your medical history with your doctor. If your answers are acceptable, you'll go on to Phase II Testing.

Phase II Testing

This also takes place at an FBI field office. There are two parts, a structured interview and a written exercise.

The interview may last for an hour or more. You'll be asked questions by a team of specially trained agents. They will listen to how well you communicate ideas and information when you speak. Through their questions, the agents

The process of applying to work for the FBI must begin on a computer, but a substantial part of it takes place through written examinations and interviews.

will try to learn about your honesty, your motivation, and how you adapt to changing conditions.

In the written exercise, you'll be given some notes and graphs about something that has happened or may happen soon. From this, you'll have to write a report that describes the situation in detail. You'll also need to suggest what should be done about the situation and give reasons for your recommendations.

FAST FACTS

During the application process, you'll be asked some questions again and again, both on forms and in interviews. This is a basic investigative technique. The Bureau wants to make sure you give the same answer each time.

Conditional Appointment

For Phase II activities, like Phase I, you either pass or fail. If you pass, you will receive a conditional appointment as an FBI special agent. "Conditional" means the appointment is only good if you successfully complete the final steps in the application process.

The Final Steps

Three to six weeks after you pass Phase II Testing, you'll be called back to an FBI field office for a Personal Security Interview (PSI). You'll be asked questions about your work history, drinking and drug use, money matters, and more. Your answers to the interview questions may be tested on the next step: the polygraph.

The polygraph, or lie detector test, is often given right after the PSI. You'll be connected to the machine and asked a series of questions about security and criminal issues. Your answers will be checked against your responses to earlier written and interview questions.

FAST FACTS

Before beginning Phase II testing, you must sign a "non-disclosure" form. This is a promise that you won't tell anyone about the questions you're asked. Your interview will be recorded and the tape sent to FBI headquarters in Washington.

In the time between Phase I and Phase II, you will also be the subject of a background investigation. FBI personnel will visit your friends, relatives, co-workers, and bosses. They will ask questions about your honesty, reliability, judgment, and loyalty.

You will also have a thorough medical examination. This determines if you are healthy enough to participate in training and to serve as a special agent. Part of the medical exam is blood and urine testing for the use of illegal drugs. There are height and weight requirements, and you must have excellent hearing and vision—though you may wear glasses or contact lenses.

Last, but certainly not least, is the physical fitness test. It is made up of four events: push-ups, sit-ups, a 330-yard (300-meter) sprint, and a 1.5-mile (2.4-kilometer) run. There are different passing standards for men and women, but they are rigorous. The Bureau demands a high level of strength and fitness for both agents and trainees.

A Date at Quantico

Completing all of the testing, interviews, and exams can take a year or longer. If you are successful, you'll get a letter telling you when to report for New Agent Training. This is held at the FBI Academy, in Quantico, Virginia.

Polygraph tests are not infallible, but they can provide insights into a candidate's reactions to a number of questions that might otherwise be difficult to obtain.

THE POLYGRAPH TEST

When you go to the doctor, someone usually checks your pulse. They'll put a finger or two on your wrist and count heart beats for 60 seconds. That measures your pulse for just one minute. Now imagine checking your pulse constantly for an hour or more. Your heart rate would speed up or slow down depending on what was happening to you. That's the idea behind the polygraph, commonly known as a lie detector.

The first modern polygraph was built by John A. Larson in 1921. His machine could track a person's blood pressure, pulse, and breathing rates all at once and for long periods of time. Larson's idea was that a person's body acts differently when he or she is telling a lie. The person may speak convincingly, but his or her pulse or blood pressure will change.

When a person is tested, he or she is first asked simple, obvious questions, such as name, eye color, and birth date. This creates a "baseline" of measurements, showing how the person's body acts when telling the truth. These measurements are then compared to the person's reactions later on, when he or she may be asked about drug use or crimes.

Some **psychologists** say polygraph tests are not always accurate. Some judges do not allow them as **evidence** in court. Even so, police and security agencies have been using them since 1924. Everyone who receives a conditional appointment as a special agent must pass a polygraph test.

CHAPTER 3
Books, Bullets, and Boxing Gloves

The red brick buildings are connected by glass-covered walkways. Some of the buildings hold classrooms or offices. There are dormitories with smallish rooms, coin-operated washing machines, and lounge areas with couches, TV sets, and video games. There's a big library, a gym and track, and a cafeteria. It seems like a college campus, except for one thing. There is an almost constant sound of gunfire. This is Quantico, home of the FBI Academy.

Welcome to Quantico

The Academy is on the grounds of a large U.S. Marine Corps base in Quantico, Virginia, not far from Washington, D.C. Years ago, the Bureau used Quantico only for firearms training. All other instruction was done in Washington. But in 1972, the Academy expanded its training and moved all of it to Quantico. The facilities have continued to expand and improve ever since.

Since the FBI moved its training academy to Quantico in 1972, it has looked more like a college campus than a military base.

Quantico has long been the home of FBI firearms training. Today's sessions are likely to focus on individual as well as group instruction. In this photo, a NAT (New Agent Trainee) practices firing a handgun under the supervision of an instructor.

Training groups—simply called classes—are small, ranging from 30 to a maximum of 50 people. For many activities, however, New Agent Trainees (**NATs**) are divided into smaller groups. This does two things. First, it gives trainees as much individual instruction as possible. Second, it allows instructors to better evaluate each trainee's performance and abilities.

Uniforms and Curfews

The new-agent training program lasts for 18 weeks. During that time, NATs live in the Quantico dormitories. They wear a standard uniform of khaki pants, dark blue polo shirts, and hiking boots. Their typical day goes from 8:00 A.M. to 5:00 P.M., but there are few "typical" days. Trainees very often spend the early morning and evening hours studying, working out, or both.

The standard uniform of dark blue polo shirts. khaki pants, and hiking boots clearly distinguishes NATs as both FBI employees and trainees.

For the first two weeks, trainees may not leave the Academy campus. After that, they may leave at night and on weekends. There is, however, an enforced midnight **curfew**. Trainees who are not doing as well as expected may lose their "off campus" privileges, and may have to put in extra training time until their work improves.

A Contract

Technically, NATs are already FBI employees, but training is really the final step of the hiring process. One of the first things NATs do when they arrive at Quantico is sign a contract. This document is 20 pages long and lists everything expected of both the Bureau and the trainee. A NAT may be dismissed if he or she fails to live up to the terms of the contract.

The most common reason for dismissal is physical fitness. Tests are given in the first, seventh, and fourteenth weeks of training. Failing two of these tests may be grounds for dismissal. Poor **academic** performance may also lead to dismissal. An FBI training official said, "We cram four years of college into four months." Trainees who don't take their classroom work seriously don't become special agents.

Thomas H. Ackerman, who had a long career with the FBI, wrote,

The New Agents Training program is designed to push trainees' minds and bodies to their limits, leaving them with new tools, a few dozen close friends, and a keen sense of accomplishment.

Hitting the Books

FBI special agents are charged with investigating crimes that violate federal laws—that means laws that apply to all of the United States. These are often different from state laws, and agents must know those differences. Classroom topics include criminal law, constitutional law, the laws of arrest, and laws about admissions and confessions. Not everything an arrested person or suspect says can be used in court.

NATs spend up to 70 hours studying interviewing and **interrogation** tech-

REALITY CHECK

During the first week of each training program, an instructor carries out what the Bureau calls a "reality check." The idea is to remind the trainees that they have signed up for a potentially life-threatening job. In 2006, instructor Thomas Hauber demonstrated this point by showing his class some pistols. One of them had a hole in it. It had belonged to a special agent who was killed in a gun battle. Another pistol was partly melted. It had belonged to a special agent who rushed into the World Trade Center in New York on September 11, 2001, and never made it out. "You are volunteering to put yourself in harm's way," Hauber told the class. "When everyone is running away from danger, you must run toward it."

niques. These are extremely important. FBI agents spend a lot of time talking to witnesses, informants, and suspects. Actors are sometimes used to play these people, and the trainee's sessions with them are videotaped for later discussion.

FAST FACTS

Edwin C. Shanahan was the first FBI Agent killed in the line of duty. He was murdered by a car thief in 1925.

Top: an FBI counterterrorism/hostage-rescue exercise. Bottom: the FBI's *Handbook of Forensic Services.* Both areas—counterterrorism and forensics—have grown in importance as the United States finds itself on higher levels of national security alert and as the processing of clues has become more sophisticated in the age of high-tech digital analysis.

Classes also cover topics such as the following:

- counterterrorism
- national security and intelligence
- **forensic** sciences
- computer skills, data analysis, and information security
- financial investigation tools and techniques
- behavioral sciences
- drug identification
- international investigations
- telephone records analysis
- case management

New agents must pass nine academic tests with a score of 85 percent or better. Those include two exams in legal matters. The classes are all taught by experts. Some of them are current or former agents. Others are college professors, bankers, psychologists, officers from the Drug Enforcement Agency, or technical experts.

Getting Strong

FBI physical training focuses on overall health, nutrition, muscular strength, flexibility, and endurance. Training includes a lot of running, weight training, and stretching. There's also "the yellow brick road." This is a 6-mile (9.6-km) obstacle course that includes hurdles, rope climbing, and barbed wire.

The same physical fitness test applicants must pass to reach the Academy is given three more times during training. Points are given for each of the four events, on a scale from 10 to minus 2. To pass, the trainee must score at least one point in each area, and a total of at least 12 points. This chart shows what men and women must do to score three points in each event:

Included in the rigorous obstacle course ironically referred to as "the yellow brick road" is a set of ropes constructed to make a net that tests trainees' sure-footedness.

	MEN	WOMEN
push-ups	40–43	22–26
sit-ups (1 minute)	43–44	41–42
300-meter sprint	48.0–49.4 sec.	57.5–59.9 sec.
1.5-mile run	11:10–11:34 min.	12:30–12:59 min.

Defending Yourself

At the Academy, the use of physical strength to protect one-self or subdue someone else is called defensive tactics. Trainees learn kicks and punches, special holds to keep suspects under control, arrest procedures, and handcuffing. All trainees themselves are handcuffed for periods of time so they know what it's like and how a handcuffed suspect might be expected to react.

Every trainee also goes through "the OC test." "OC" stands for *oleoresin capsicum*, commonly called pepper spray. During the test, one NAT tries to "arrest" another and gets a blast of pepper spray right in the eyes. To pass the test, the sprayed trainee must protect his or her gun so it's not taken away and force the "bad guy" trainee onto the ground. Instructors want NATs to know what OC spray feels like before they use it on someone else. They also want them to learn that they can still function if it's used against them.

Handcuffing training. Subduing and cuffing a struggling, resistant suspect takes a great deal of skill and composure.

The Bull Ring

Many (often most) trainees have never been in a fight. Academy instructors use an exercise called "Bull in the Ring" to give them that experience. NATs are divided into groups according to weight. Each group forms a circle, with one person in the center. Everyone wears boxing gloves, headgear, and mouth guards. One by one, those in the circle attack the person in the middle. The fighting may go on for several minutes, and the instructors don't allow faking. The attackers are told to hit hard.

Exercises like this are serious. People can get hurt. But it is through these activities that trainees learn how to survive and defend themselves. John Kerr, the chief of Quantico's physical training unit, once said, "If you're going to be on the street, things could happen to you and you have to be prepared."

FAST FACTS

In the course of their firearms instruction at Quantico, each New Agent Trainee fires 3,000 to 5,000 rounds of ammunition. Bullets usually cost at least 40 cents each.

Firearms

Many new agent trainees have never fired a gun. The Bureau demands that they become expert marksmen. Trainees begin by firing at stationary paper targets. They learn to shoot their pistols with both hands at once, and with each hand individually. The preferred way of shooting is with two hands, but in a gunfight, an agent may be wounded in the hand or arm. He or she must be able to keep firing accurately with the other hand.

NATS training in the use of handguns (below) check their targets to see how they performed (right).

Trainees learn to use a shotgun and a submachine gun, but most of their time is spent with the Bureau-issued handgun. This is usually a .40 caliber or 9 mm automatic. They are tested with it three times. For their final pistol exam, trainees must fire from four positions at four distances—150 shots in all. To pass, at least 120 shots must hit the target.

NATs are also taught combat survival shooting. In movies, you may see FBI agents standing in the middle of a street, blazing away at the bad guys. That's not how the Bureau really does it. Trainees are taught to use all possible cover and concealment during a gun battle. They're taught to hide behind cars, fire hydrants, mail boxes, and trees.

Weapons and Judgment

Trainees also spend a lot of time with the Firearms Automated Training System (FATS). This is like a video game, but it is deadly serious. Each trainee stands in front of a large video screen with an electronic pistol in its holster. Different

In this photo from the "gangster" era of the 1930s, an agent is training to fire a handgun from a car. In today's FBI, agents must also be able
to fire weapons accurately from moving vehicles.

scenes appear on the screen, showing all sorts of people in
all sorts of situations. For example, the video may simulate
a raid on a suspected drug house. Someone pops out of a
doorway holding a gun. Is it a drug dealer or an undercover
agent? The trainee must decide and act instantly. FATS tests
trainees' judgment, reaction time, and shooting accuracy.

Guidance Counselors

Each class of trainees has counselors to guide them. They
are experienced special agents who volunteer to work with
the NATs. During the 18-week program, counselors live in the
same dormitories as the trainees. Becoming a special agent
is a serious undertaking. NATs sometimes question their
decision partway through training. The counselors give them
someone to talk to who has experienced the same sort of
problem. Counselors also act as teachers, coaches, or—if nec-
essary—disciplinarians.

CHAPTER 4 Into the Alley

You didn't learn to ride a bicycle by watching films and reading manuals. You learned by getting on the bike and riding (maybe with a little help in the beginning from a grown-up or training wheels). You mastered those two wheels out on the sidewalks and streets.

The FBI faced the same sort of training problem more than 20 years ago. New agents weren't learning enough about working on the streets. "Crime doesn't unfold in a classroom," said Jim Pledger, a long-time special agent and training instructor. "We realized we could no longer limit ourselves to a square brick building."

So the FBI decided to take its training beyond the classroom and firing range, and out into the streets. The problem was finding some streets they could use.

Hollywood Help

In the end, the Bureau built its own streets, buildings, and neighborhoods. A lot of money was spent to create a realistic town that could be used to train

special agents. Hollywood movie set designers were hired to help with the project. FBI agents and instructors provided ideas. The result was Hogan's Alley, a version of a small American town that opened on the grounds of the FBI Academy in 1987.

Hogan's Alley has a bank, drugstore, barbershop, and pool hall. There's a bar called The Pastime, a Greyhound bus station, a deli, a court house, and residential streets. The town

Hogan's Alley. Shown here (from left): a camera operator filming a training exercise in front of the "movie theater"; a "townhouse" on the corner of a "residential" street; an "interior" with agents performing a "clear" exercise; and a "used car lot," complete with the types of slogan you'd expect at a place called "Honest Jim's."

WHAT'S AT THE MOVIES?

Nearly everything at the Academy is a reminder of the FBI's mission or its history. In 1934, a bank robber named John Dillinger was the most wanted criminal in the United States. He was called "public enemy number one." That year, FBI agents cornered Dillinger as he was coming out of a movie theater in Chicago. He tried to escape but was shot and killed. The movie theater in Hogan's Alley is called the Biograph. That was the name of the theater where Dillinger was killed. Posters at the theater advertise a film called "Manhattan Melodrama" (below), with Clark Gable and Myrna Loy. That was the movie Dillinger watched that night in 1934.

The FBI has created an ingenious case of art imitating life in its selection of a real-life model for its fake movie house in Hogan's Alley. The Hogan's Alley version is shown above. Shown below: the real-life street scene that unfolded only hours after agents had gunned down "public enemy number one" John Dillinger as he left the Biograph in Chicago. A newspaper held by a woman bears a headline reading "Dillinger Slain."

has a movie theater, a coin-operated laundromat, and a motel called the Dogwood Inn. Cars and trucks (all of them taken from real crime scenes) are parked on the streets.

FAST FACTS

The FBI actually runs two training schools at Quantico. The FBI Academy has trained new agents for the Bureau since 1928. The National Academy, set up in 1935, trains state and local police officers in modern investigation methods.

There are different stories about where the name of the town came from. Some say it's from a comic strip called "Hogan's Alley" that ran in newspapers in the 1890s. Others say it comes from a video game, also called "Hogan's Alley," that was released by Nintendo in 1984.

Informers, Terrorists, and Lawyers

Hogan's Alley is populated by actors. Some of them are professionals. Others are off-duty FBI agents, college students, lawyers, teachers on school breaks, or wives of Marines from the base next door. As realistically as they can, these people act out their roles as crime victims, drug dealers, informants, terrorists, hostages, and defense attorneys.

Every day there are shootings. Telephones are **tapped**. Drug dealers are arrested. Terrorists are spied upon. Criminal cases are tried in court. Agents say that Hogan's Alley is the most crime-ridden town in the United States. With Hogan's Alley, the FBI has definitely taken its training out of those square brick buildings and into the streets.

The Integrated Case Scenario

The FBI tries to solve crimes by using logical, step-by-step procedures. Information is collected, analyzed, and acted upon. New agents are trained the same way. They are taught something, they learn more about it, and then they practice it.

That approach is the idea behind the Integrated Case Scenario (ICS). As new agents go through their training, they learn about law, interviewing witnesses, surveillance, making arrests, and testifying in court. The ICS teaches them to put these things together to solve a crime. The scenario is played out in classrooms, in the gym, and on the streets of Hogan's Alley.

Terrorist Telephone

Here's an example of how it works. Early in their training program, a team of NATs is assigned to a case. In the beginning, the case may not seem like much. It may be just a copy of some telephone bills.

In their investigative techniques classes, the team will be asked to examine the bills. Using telephone directories and the Internet, the team learns that several calls were made to and received from a country in the Middle East that supports terrorism. Next, team members contact the telephone company, but they must **verify** their identity before they can get any information. Once they do, the trainees learn that the phone is located in an apartment above the pool hall in Hogan's Alley.

Laws and Listening Posts

In legal classes, the team will be asked if, according to U.S. laws, these telephone records could be used in court. Were they obtained legally?

Based on the evidence and current laws, will a judge authorize a "tap" on the telephone? With help from instructors, the team puts together the paperwork that a judge will need to make a decision. They take their documents to the Court House in Hogan's Alley. There, a "judge" (played by an actor) issues a court order giving the team permission to tap the phone.

Lectures and demonstrations show team members how to tap different kinds of telephones. The trainees accompany an FBI technician who places a "bug" in the apartment phone. A listening post is set up in a room at the Dogwood Inn. There, team members listen to the conversations on the telephone belonging to the "suspect" and capture them on tape recorders. Parts of the conversations are in a

FAST FACTS

The Academy has a 1.1-mile (2.7-km) driving track where trainees learn defensive and pursuit driving techniques.

John Piro, shown here on the CBS news magazine *60 Minutes*, is a Lebanese-born special agent and Bureau linguist who is fluent in Arabic. He was assigned to interview Saddam Hussein following the deposed Iraqi dictator's capture in December 2003. Thanks to Agent Piro's skills as a translator and interviewer, he was able to create a bond of trust with Saddam, who then offered Piro information that was valuable to U.S. forces.

foreign language. Bureau linguists are brought in to translate the tapes.

The Classroom and the Gym

The case progresses as the trainees learn. They study surveillance techniques. Photographic technicians show the team how to use various types of still and video cameras. Members take turns following their "suspect" through the buildings and streets of the town. Some of this is done on foot, some in cars.

Back in the classroom, NATs review the legal procedures for arresting someone, including the amount of force that may be used and the rights of the suspect. In the gym, the team practices arrest and handcuffing procedures. The next day, they "arrest" the man who lives in the apartment above the pool hall.

An agent practices the procedures used for arresting a suspect in this Hogan's Alley hallway.

Making It Real

Integrated Case Scenarios force NATs to climb into dumpsters looking for evidence. Trainees take fingerprints from broken bottles and send them to FBI headquarters. They make written and verbal reports of their activities. There may be gun battles (using blank ammunition) on the streets of Hogan's Alley. Everything is made as real as possible. Trainees' actions are closely watched and evaluated each step of the way.

Nancy Traver, a writer for *Time* magazine, observed parts of an ICS. Here is what she wrote about it:

FAST FACTS

The FBI has its own police force. Members wear uniforms, carry firearms, and ride in cars that say "FBI Police" on the sides. They are not special agents, but they are federal law enforcement officers. Their job is to protect FBI facilities and employees.

A street scene at Hogan's Alley. Here, agents working under true-to-life circumstances are trained to use body shields. In this situation, they face gunfire (from blank ammunition) coming from within a building where "suspects" are holed up.

Agents learn how to frisk suspects, read them their rights, and complete arrest forms. Instructors, all of whom are former agents, carefully critique every arrest, providing pointers on how best to subdue a struggling suspect or slip on handcuffs. No detail seems to go unnoticed. At one recent training session, a future agent was told he should go home, stand in front of his mirror and practice shouting in a forceful voice 'Freeze! This is the FBI!'

Hard Lessons Learned

Things don't always work out as trainees plan, of course. This is part of the Bureau's way of making training "real."

In a recent ICS, a team of trainees had been watching "Billy Ray Hankins," the leader of a domestic terrorist group. One member of the team went "undercover" to buy illegal weapons from Hankins. The sale was to take place in a room at the Dogwood Inn. Tiny video cameras were hidden in the room, with **monitors** and recorders in the room next door.

At just the right moment, the trainees burst into the room with guns drawn, yelling "FBI! Hands up!" While they were handcuffing the suspects, however, an instructor sneaked into the other room and stole the videotape. The trainees forgot to leave someone behind to protect their evidence. Without it, their case could not stand up in court.

Even when they get to court, near the end of most Integrated Case Scenarios, things are not easy. In the Hogan's Alley courtroom, they face actors (some of whom are real lawyers) who defend the suspect whom the team has arrested. Instructor Jim Pledger says the actors make it really hard for the trainees. Any mistake they've have made in putting together a case will become obvious in court. "We really let the sharks go after them there," he says. "Having to eat your paperwork and watch the criminals go free teaches you to do everything by the book."

Going by the book, step by logical step, is the FBI way.

LIKE THE MARINES NEXT DOOR

Joseph W. Koletar, an author and former special agent, says it's appropriate that the FBI shares Quantico with the Marines. The organizations are similar in many ways. He writes:

> Each is but a small part of a much larger component. The Marine Corps is part of the U.S. Navy and the FBI is part of the U.S. Justice Department.... Each is a demanding environment, chockfull of myths and legends. Each is highly selective about who it recruits. Each has a demanding training cycle and little tolerance for deviation from its rules and regulations... Each is looked to by the citizens of the United States to perform difficult, complex, and dangerous missions.

Being a special agent means more than just getting the "bad guys." It includes facing lawyers, judges, and juries. In Hogan's Alley, trainees learn the critical importance of following the rules in obtaining evidence and making arrests so that what they have worked so hard to achieve holds up in court.

5 On the Job

The big day comes after weeks and weeks of intense physical and mental effort. The NATs are no longer wearing blue polo shirts and boots. They're wearing dark business suits, dresses, and polished shoes. They are gathered in the main auditorium at Quantico. One at a time, as their families watch, they walk across the stage to receive their **credentials**. They've made it. They are now FBI special agents.

After congratulations and photos, the new special agents walk across the Academy campus to the gun vault. There, each of them receives his or her line-of-duty handgun.

Receiving an FBI badge and handgun at the end of training is a huge honor and the culmination of a rigorous application process and training program. With them also come the tremendous responsibility of upholding and enforcing federal laws.

Orders

When graduation ceremonies are over, the new agents leave for their assignments. In a traditional ceremony during training called "Orders," they had learned which field office they'd be reporting to.

During the Orders ceremony, each trainee stands before the class. One at a time they are given a sealed envelope with their assignment. The trainee must read out the posting, find its location on a giant map of the United States, and then pin his or her picture to the map.

Like everything else in the FBI, there is a purpose behind the ceremony. First, it reminds the trainees that they must obey their orders, without complaining. Second, it says clearly that, as agents, they are charged with enforcing all federal laws, all across the United States. Agents in Washington or Los

MOVIE PEOPLE, REAL PEOPLE

The 1991 movie *The Silence of the Lambs* is often named as one of the best movies about the FBI. In the film, Jodie Foster plays a trainee named Clarice Starling, who helps track down a serial killer played by Anthony Hopkins. At the end of the film, Starling graduates from training as an FBI special agent. When she receives her credentials in the film, the man presenting them is Tony Daniels. He was the real Assistant Director of the FBI Academy at the time. Several other real FBI officials are in the scene as well.

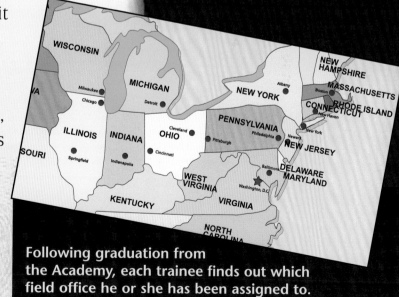

Following graduation from the Academy, each trainee finds out which field office he or she has been assigned to.

47

Angeles may work on cases that make the news. Those working in Buffalo or Kansas City may not. But the Orders ceremony says that all federal laws are important, and that every case in every city must be treated the same way.

Reporting for Work

Each FBI field office is headed by a Special Agent in Charge, or SAC (sometimes—though not in public—called "the sack"). The SAC decides where to place the new agent. In larger field offices, agents are assigned to various squads, each of which has specific duties. New agents are frequently assigned to the squad that does background investigations on people who are applying to the FBI. It's a good place to start. First, it helps new agents learn the city or area to which they've been assigned. Second, they get to practice investigative skills safely.

Probation

New agents are "on **probation**" for their first two years of service. During this time, each agent's work is reviewed by a supervisory agent. This person will guide the new agent in assignments, point out mistakes and how to correct them, and do whatever is needed to help the new agent succeed. The supervisor will also help the new agent with "adjustment" issues, like finding a

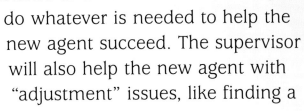

New agents reporting for duty to the FBI's Milwaukee Division in 1979 were in on a historic moment. On February 16, John D. Glover became Special Agent in Charge (SAC) of that division, making him the first African American to head a Bureau field office.

place to live or buy clothes. Clothes are important. Agents—men and women alike—wear suits on duty. Unless they're undercover or on a special assignment, there are no exceptions to the dress code.

Field offices have a record book called a Probationary Agent Log. It lists tasks a new agent should perform during the first two years of service, including making arrests, testifying in court, and filling out a variety of reports. It is the responsibility of the supervisor to see that the new agent accomplishes as many of these tasks as possible.

FAST FACTS

People used to stand in long lines to visit FBI headquarters in Washington, D.C. All tours included law enforcement technology, the Bureau's huge collection of firearms, and a shooting demonstration by FBI instructors. The tours were stopped after the attacks of 9/11. Many Washington visitors hope they will begin again soon.

Each of these agents started off wearing the same "NAT" uniform—blue polo shirt, khaki pants, and hiking boots. As full-fledged special agents, their usual mode of dress is now strictly business.

The supervisor also reports on the new agent's perform-ance to the SAC. If the agent's work is consistent-ly poor, he or she may be dismissed.

Keep Learning, Keep Practicing

An agent may complete training, but that doesn't mean that learning is finished. All special agents are required to complete at least 15 hours of in-service train-ing every year. This training may cover national security, changes to federal laws, or a refresher class in first-aid. Many agents also learn useful new skills—such as a foreign language or scuba diving—on their own.

Agents are tested with firearms several times a year. Some experienced agents carry personal firearms instead of Bureau-issued pistols. If so, they must pass shooting tests with both weapons.

Other Jobs with the FBI

Suppose you like the idea of work-ing for the FBI, but you have a situ-

FAST FACTS

The FBI has its own air force. The Bureau has nearly 100 aircraft and 300 pilots. Pilots are usually high on the Bureau's "most wanted" employee list.

Agents are required to maintain their physical fitness through regular workouts.

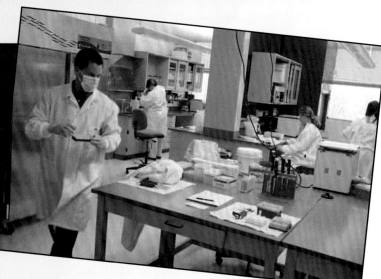

Non-agent lab workers at the FBI's new forensics and evidence lab facility in Quantico. This lab employs people with backgrounds in biology, physiology, and other natural sciences. Their work includes extracting and analyzing DNA.

ation that will prevent you from becoming a special agent. Perhaps your eyesight isn't good enough to pass the medical exam. Or you're too short or can't run fast enough to pass the fitness test. Well, the good news is that you don't have to be a special agent to work for the Bureau. In fact, fewer than half of the Bureau's employees are agents. The others are known as professional support personnel or, as the Bureau sometimes calls them, non-agents—and they work at more than 300 different jobs.

All Sorts of Jobs

Some of those 300 jobs are ones you would expect, but others may surprise you. Here are just a few of the non-agent jobs at the FBI.

Biologists. The FBI has one of the largest and most complete forensic laboratories in the world. Biologists at these labs examine and analyze body tissues and fluids, bone, hair, and teeth. They match DNA from suspects to DNA found on clothing, cigarette butts, and even postage stamps. FBI biologists often provide expert testimony in criminal trials.

Clerical and administrative personnel. No office—including an FBI office—can run without these people. Clerical and administrative staff members keep track of records, files, and forms. They make sure office supplies are on hand, transcribe written or recorded notes, make copies, and keep track of who is where at any given time.

Physical Sciences. What kind of car did that paint come from? Is it the same as the paint on this truck? What kind of explosives made those black marks? Where does this soil come from? The FBI needs answers to questions like that. People who are trained in physical sciences such as chemistry, physics, and geology can answer them.

The FBI has response teams that can begin the process of collecting, sorting, and analyzing evidence and turning it into scientific data at the point where it is freshest and most reliable—the scene of the crime. These units are staffed by scientists and technicians with backgrounds in chemistry and other physical sciences.

Electronics technicians. These "techies" install and maintain the communications and security systems in FBI field offices. These systems include computers, phones, and fax systems; all sorts of transmitters and receivers; the radios and electronics used in FBI cars; and field surveillance equipment such as video cameras and audio devices.

The Bureau relies on photographic evidence as the basis for many reconstructions and analyses of crime scenes.

Fingerprint specialists. The FBI has the world's largest collection of fingerprints. In addition to 219 million fingerprint cards, the Bureau has large and sophisticated computer **databases** that include fingerprints, footprints, palm prints, and even lip prints. Bureau specialists visit crime scenes to find, collect, analyze and preserve prints. In disasters, such as the space shuttle *Challenger* explosion in 1986, fingerprint specialists even help identify victims.

Photographers. The FBI likes pictures. Photographers are used

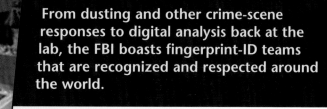

From dusting and other crime-scene responses to digital analysis back at the lab, the FBI boasts fingerprint-ID teams that are recognized and respected around the world.

at nearly every crime scene. Their pictures may show crime victims. They also show evidence found at the crime scene and show where objects were in relation to other objects. Photographers also conduct or assist with photo surveillance of suspects who may be engaged in criminal activity. Some of them take photos from aircraft.

Qualifying for a Non-Agent Job

Everyone who works for the FBI—agent or non-agent—must be a U.S. citizen. Most of the non-agent positions require at least a four-year college degree. The Bureau also requires considerable work experience in the area of the job in question. The exact requirements, of course, vary according to the job.

FAST FACTS

The Bureau's Strategic Intelligence Operations Center (SIOC) is in the Hoover Building (shown below at night) in Washington, D.C. It is used in emergencies and to direct special cases. The SIOC has 1,100 telephone lines, 235 computer terminals, and 60 miles (96.5 km) of fiber optic cable.

The Application and Hiring Process

The process is similar to applying to be a special agent. You must submit an online application that includes personal information, education, and work history. If you qualify to move to the next step, you'll take written exams in your area of expertise (if you say you can read and write Japanese, you'll be asked to do so). Like special agent applicants, you must complete the SF-86 National Security Questionnaire and go through a personal interview. If you make it that far, you'll go through the final steps: a background investigation, security interview, polygraph, drug testing, and a pre-employment physical. Most non-agent applicants do not have to take the physical fitness test.

Diversity

At one time, the FBI was almost exclusively made up of white men. But no more. Diversity is an important part of FBI hiring practices. Of the 30,000 people who work for the FBI, nearly 8,000 are minorities, and 1,100 are people with disabilities. More than 13,000 are women.

As this group of photos from the FBI's Web site suggests, the Bureau wants to attract a diverse work force.

Remembering Priorities

Whether you work for the FBI as a special agent or as part of the professional support team,

FBI and other personnel monitor the inauguration of President Barack Obama at a command center in January 2009. The Secret Service is responsible for the safety of the president of the United States and takes the lead in providing security for presidential inaugurations. The FBI's presence is crucial, however, in matters involving national security and the threat of terrorism.

the Bureau constantly reminds you of its mission and priorities. The top priority for the FBI today is protecting the United States against terrorism. One reminder of this is found at Quantico.

On the grounds of the Academy are two 10-foot (3-m) towers carved from black stone. They are shaped like the Twin Towers that once stood at the World Trade Center. On the ground below them are a jagged piece of stone taken from Ground Zero at the World Trade Center, a piece of concrete from the shattered wall of the Pentagon, and a scrap of blue metal, taken from the remains of Flight 93, the hijacked airplane that crashed in Pennsylvania on September 11, 2001.

These items, in place as they are as part of a sculpture at the Bureau's training facility, serve as a reminder that the FBI remembers its mission and its priorities.

CHRONOLOGY

1908: Attorney General Charles Bonaparte assembles a group of "special agents" to investigate federal crimes.

1909: The team of special agents is named the Bureau of Investigation.

1914: World War I begins. The Bureau investigates spies.

1919: New federal laws give Bureau agents more powers to pursue criminals across state borders.

1924: The Bureau's Fingerprints Division is created.

1925: Edwin C. Shanahan becomes the first Bureau agent killed in the line of duty.

The Bureau opens a training school for new agents.

1932: The Bureau of Investigation is renamed the U.S. Bureau of Investigation.

The Bureau's Crime Laboratory is established.

1933: The U.S. Bureau of Investigation becomes the Division of Investigation.

1934: Special agents are authorized to carry firearms for the first time.

1935: The organization is officially renamed the Federal Bureau of Investigation.

The FBI National Academy is founded to train state and local police investigators.

1941: The United States enters World War II on December 7.

The FBI rounds up resident aliens from Italy, Germany, and Japan.

1945: World War II ends.

The FBI starts investigating U.S. government and defense industry employees, looking for communists.

1950: The FBI's "Ten Most Wanted" list is published for the first time.

1964: New civil rights laws are passed. Bureau agents work to enforce the rights of African Americans.

1972: J. Edgar Hoover dies.

The new FBI Academy opens in Quantico, Virginia.

1987: Hogan's Alley, the Bureau's "training town," opens at Quantico.

1999: Terrorist leader Osama Bin Laden is placed on the FBI's "Ten Most Wanted" list.

2001: Terrorists hijack four commercial airliners on September 11. They attack the World Trade Center in New York City with two of them and the Pentagon near Washington, D.C. The fourth crashes into a field in Pennsylvania following a struggle for control of the plane between the terrorists and passengers and crew members.

Identifying and fighting the threat of terrorism becomes the Bureau's top priority.

2008: The FBI celebrates its 100th anniversary.

GLOSSARY

academic—having to do with school or learning.

attorney general—the highest-ranking law enforcement official in the United States.

civil rights—the rights that a government guarantees to its citizens.

Cold War—a period of tension and military competition between the United States and the former Soviet Union, starting in about 1945 (at the end of World War II) and easing up in the late 1980s and ending in 1991 with the breaking up of the Soviet Union into a group of independent nations, including Russia, Georgia, Kazakhstan, Armenia, Lithuania, and Ukraine.

communism—a political and economic system in which most property is owned and controlled by the government.

counterintelligence—an activity by one agency that aims to block another agency from getting information. Counterintelligence is also used to deceive enemies with false information and to prevent acts of sabotage.

counterterrorism—actions and information used to stop terrorism and capture terrorists.

credentials—documents that prove one's identity. FBI credentials include a certificate and a badge.

curfew—a specific time when people must be indoors or at home.

cyber crime—a crime committed in a computer network or by using computer technology.

database—a large, organized collection of information stored in a computer system.

espionage—spying to steal government secrets.

evidence—material used to uncover truth or to prove guilt in a crime.

federal—having to do with the national government.

forensic—having to do with the use of scientific methods to investigate crime.

fraud—intentionally tricking someone, often as part of a plan to get his or her money.

identity theft—acquiring and misusing people's identifying information, such as their social security number, for the purpose of illegally obtaining money or credit.

intelligence—information collected about possible threats or enemies.

interrogation—intense questioning of a person, often to find out if a crime has been committed.

monitor—a television-like screen used with a computer.

NAT—abbreviation for New Agent Trainee.

probation—a period of time when a person's behavior, skills, or qualifications are tested.

Prohibition—a rule that forbids or prevents something; a time in the United States (1919–1933) when making and selling alcohol was illegal.

psychologist—an expert in the way the mind works and the ways people behave.

saboteurs—people who intentionally damage property such as factories, highways, or military equipment.

surveillance—intense and usually secret watching of people or activities.

tap—short for "wiretap"; to use a device (also called a "tap" or "wiretap") that breaks in on a telephone wire to enable people to listen to conversations held on the line.

undercover—pretending to be a criminal or a member of a criminal group in order to learn about their activities.

verify—to prove that something is true or accurate.

FURTHER READING

Ackerman, Thomas H. *FBI Careers*. Indianapolis: JIST Works, 2006.

De Capua, Sarah. *The FBI*. New York: Children's Press, 2007.

Gaines, Ann. *Special Agent and Careers in the FBI*. Berkeley Heights, NJ: Enslow Publishers, Incorporated, 2006.

Keeley, Jennifer. *Deterring and Investigating Attack: The Role of the FBI and CIA*. Farmington Hills, MI: Gale Group, 2003.

Ramaprian, Sheela. *FBI*. Danbury, CT: Children's Press, 2003.

Thomas, William D. *Working in Law Enforcement*. Milwaukee: Gareth Stevens Publishing, 2006.

Wagner, Heather Lehr. *Federal Bureau of Investigation*. Langhorne, PA: Chelsea House Publishers, 2007.

INTERNET RESOURCES

www.fbi.gov
The official Web site of the Federal Bureau of Investigation includes history, the current Most Wanted list, myths and true stories about the Bureau, and a list of all field offices.

www.fbijobs.gov
This is the place to learn about jobs with the FBI. It has information about recruiting, applying, frequently asked questions, current critical skills, and sample test questions.

www.fbi.gov/hq/td/academy/academy.htm
Check out training at Quantico for firearms, investigation, computers, forensic science, and more.

www.fbi.gov/fbikids.htm
The kids' page of the official FBI Web site offers activities and information for 6th to 12th grade students.

www.imdb.com/SearchDVD?for = fbi
Check out movies about the FBI on DVD.

The Web sites mentioned in this book were active at the time of publication. The publisher is not responsible for Web sites that have changed their addresses or discontinued operation since the date of publication. The publisher will review and update the Web site addresses each time the book is reprinted.

NOTES

Chapter 1

p. 13: "We use financial investigative techniques . . .": quoted by Nancy Traver, "Hogan's Alley, Virginia Crime," *Time*, April 30, 1990, www.time.com/printout/0,8816,969977,00.html.

p. 14: "In many cases, women possess . . .": "Female Special Agents," Federal Bureau of Investigation, www.fbijobs.gov/115.asp.

p. 15: "This is truly an opportunity . . .": Special agent "Kim," Federal Bureau of Investigation, www.fbijobs.gov/322.asp.

Chapter 2

p. 17: "We're also looking for . . .": quoted by James Vicini, "FBI Plans Large Hiring Blitz of Agents, Experts," Yahoo! News/Reuters, January 6, 2009, http://news.yahoo.com/s/nm/20090106/us_nm/us_usa_fbi_2.

p. 20: "How often are . . .": Federal Bureau of Investigation, www.fbijobs.gov/11213.asp.

p. 20: "Whenever an investigator . . .": Federal Bureau of Investigation, www.fbijobs.gov/11218.asp.

p. 21: "Your direct subordinate . . .": Federal Bureau of Investigation, www.fbijobs.gov/11215.asp.

Chapter 3

p. 28: "We cram four years of college . . .": quoted by Joseph W. Koletar, *The FBI Career Guide* (New York: Amacom, 2006), p. 165.

p. 29: "The New Agents' training program . . .": Thomas Ackerman, *FBI Careers* (Indianapolis: JIST Works, 2006), p. 209.

p. 29: "You are volunteering to put yourself . . .": quoted by Sari Horwitz, "Just Don't Quit," *Washington Post*, August 17, 2006, www.washingtonpost.com/wpdyn/content/article/2006/08/16/AR2006081601949_pf.html.

p. 33: "If you're going out on . . .": quoted by Sari Horwitz, "Just Don't Quit" *Washington Post*, August 17, 2006, www.washingtonpost.com/wpdyn/content/article/2006/08/16/AR2006081601949_pf.html.

Chapter 4

p. 36: "Crime doesn't unfold in a classroom . . .": quoted by Nancy Traver, "Hogan's Alley, Virginia Crime," *Time*, April 30, 1990, www.time.com/printout/0,8816,969977,00.html.

p. 44: "Agents learn how to frisk . . .": Ibid.

p. 45: "We really let the sharks . . .": Ibid.

p. 45: "Each is but a small part . . .": Joseph W. Koletar, *The FBI Career Guide*, p. 154.

INDEX

Numbers in **bold italics** refer to captions.

About the Author

William David Thomas lives in Rochester, New York. Bill has written books for children, software documentation, magazine articles, training programs, annual reports, lots of letters, and a few poems. His four-book series *My American Government* received an American Educational Publishers award nomination for Social Studies in 2008.